A-Z BASIN

Key to Maps

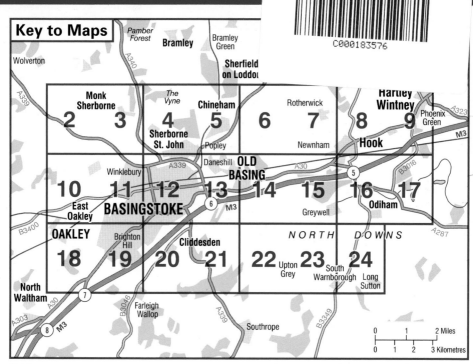

Reference

Motorway	M3	
A Road	A30	
B Road	B3400	
Dual Carriageway		
One Way Street Traffic flow on A roads is indicated by a heavy line on the drivers' left.		
Restricted Access		
Track & Footpath		
Residential Walkway		
Railway Level Crossing, Station		
Built Up Area		

Local Authority Boundary	— · —	
Postcode Boundary	— —	
Map Continuation	12	
Car Park Selected	P	
Church or Chapel	†	
Fire Station	■	
House Numbers 'A' and 'B' Roads only	47 35	
Hospital	H	
Information Centre	i	
National Grid Reference	465	
Police Station	▲	
Post Office	★	

Toilet with facilities for the Disabled	▽ ♿
Educational Establishment	
Hospital or Health Centre	
Industrial Building	
Leisure or Recreational Facility	
Place of Interest	
Public Building	
Shopping Centre or Market	
Other Selected Buildings	

Scale 1:19,000

0   ¼   ½ Mile
0   250   500   750 Metres   1 Kilometre

3⅓ inches (8.47 cm) to 1 mile
5.26 cm to 1 kilometre

Head Office:
Fairfield Road, Borough Green, Sevenoaks, Kent TN15 8PP
Tel: 01732 781000 (General Enquiries & Trade Sales)

Showrooms:
44 Gray's Inn Road, London WC1X 8HX
Tel: 020 7440 9500 (Retail Sales)
www.a-zmaps.co.uk

Ordnance Survey® This product includes mapping data licensed from Ordnance Survey® with the permission of the Controller of Her Majesty's Stationery Office.
© Crown Copyright 2001. Licence number 100017302
EDITION 1 2001   EDITION 1A 2003 (Part revision)
Copyright © Geographers' A-Z Map Co. Ltd. 2001

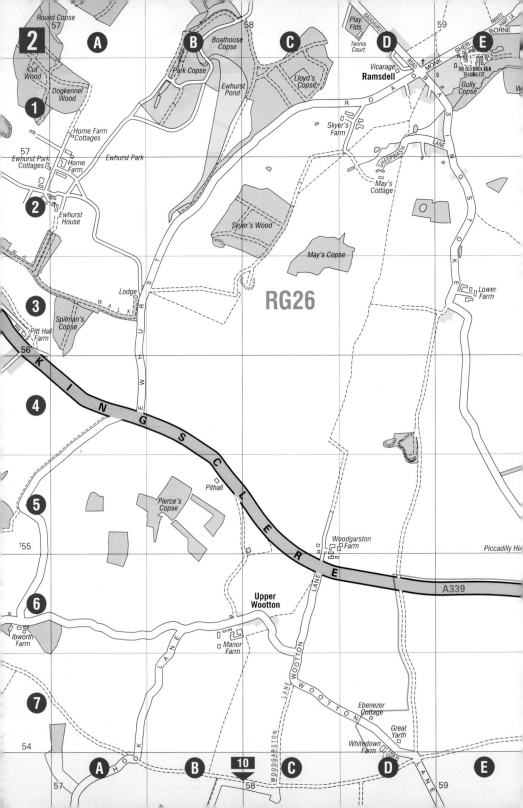

2

A · 57 · Round Copse

B · 58

C

D · Play. Flds. · Baughurst · 59 · WHITE HART LA. · BORNE

E · SHER

Cut Wood

Park Copse

Boathouse Copse

Tennis Court

Vicarage · Ramsdell

THE OLD BRICK KILN TRADING EST.

1

Dogkennel Wood

Ewhurst Pond

Lloyd's Copse

Gully Copse

Home Farm Cottages

Skyer's Farm

57 · Ewhurst Park Cottages

Home Farm

Ewhurst Park

SHEEPWASH · LANE

May's Cottage

2 · Ewhurst House

Skyer's Wood

May's Copse

Lower Farm

Lodge

RG26

3 · Spilman's Copse

56 · Pitt Hall Farm

WALKI · WHURST

KINGS

4 · KINGSCLERE

5 · Pierce's Copse

Pithall

155 · Pierce's Copse

Woodgarston Farm

Piccadilly Hil

6 · Ibworth Farm

Upper Wootton

Manor Farm

A339

7

WOOTTON · LANE

WOOTTON

Ebenezer Cottage

Great Yarth

54

HOOK · LANE

WOODGARSTON

Whitedown Farm

LANE

A · 57

B · 58 · **10**

C

D · 59

E

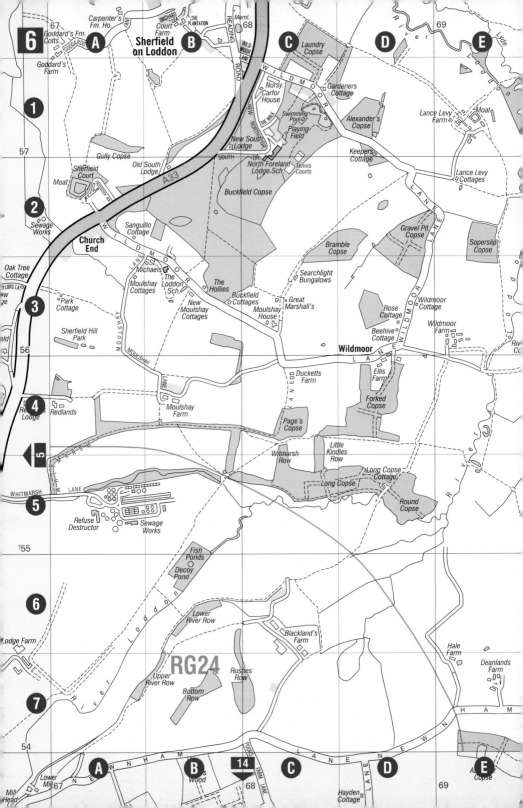

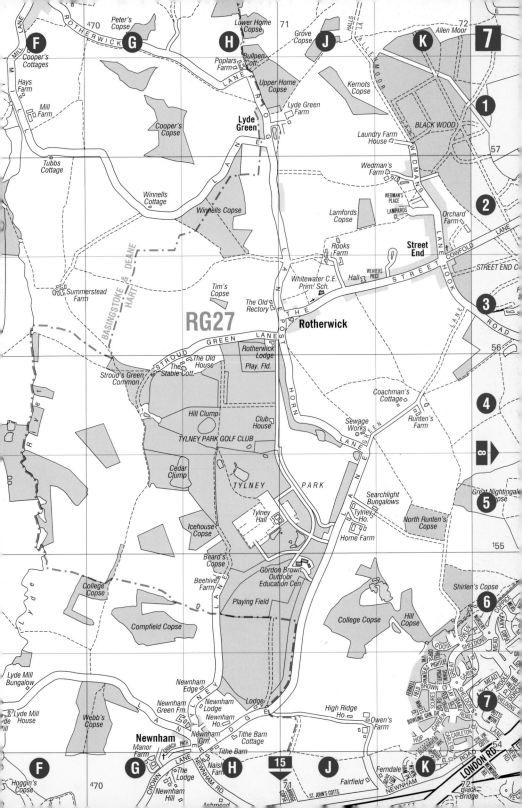

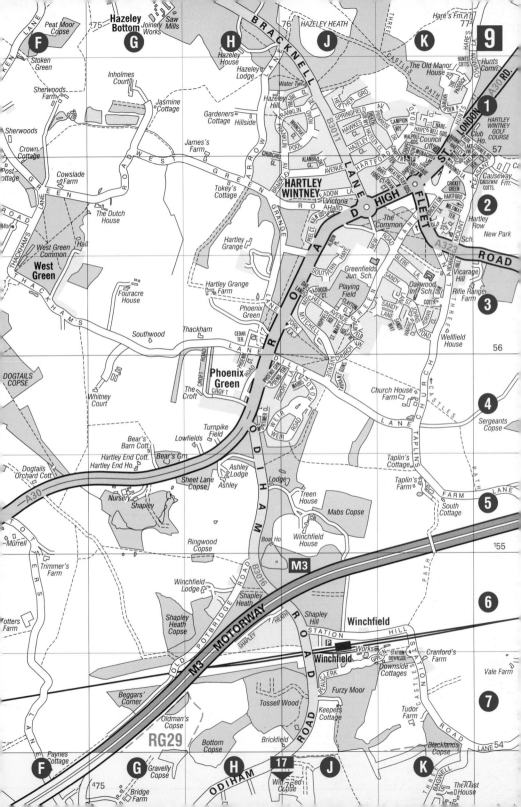

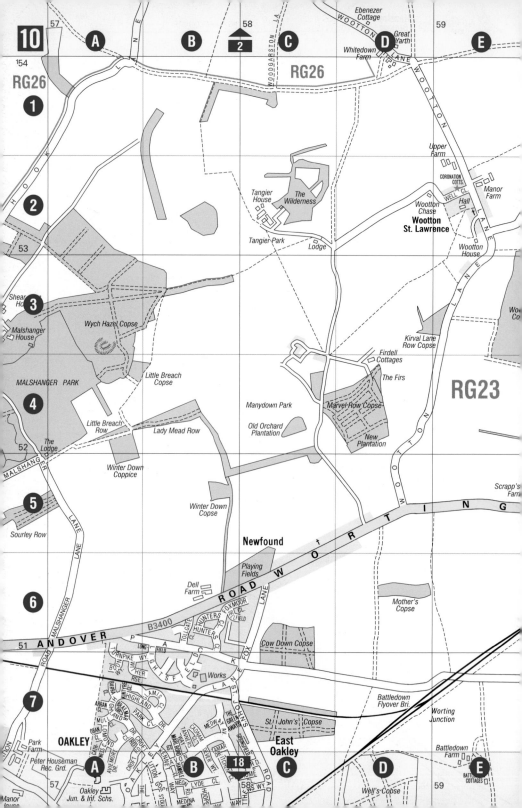

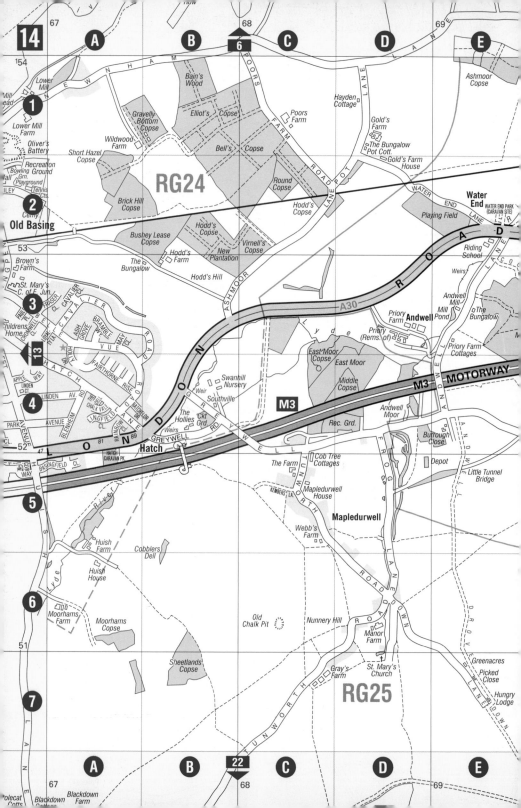

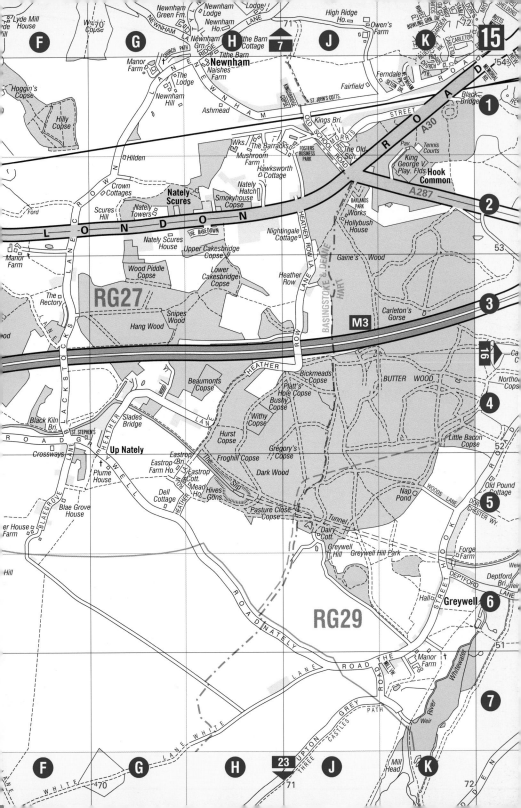

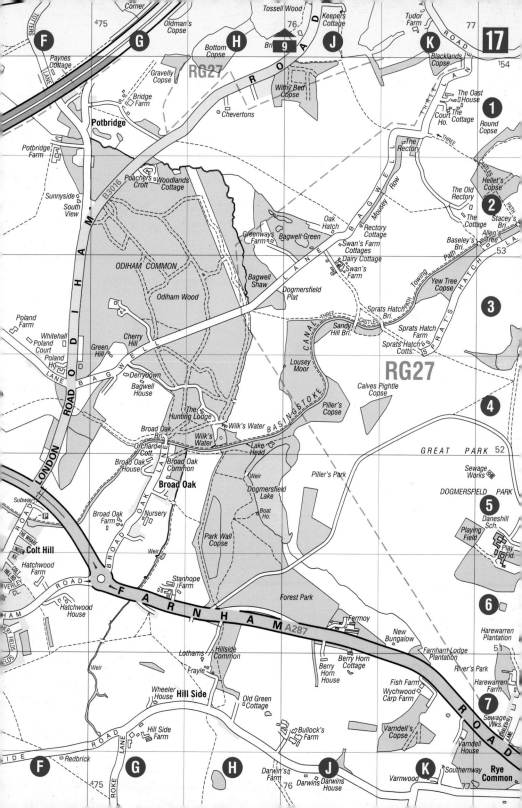

18

OAKLEY

East Oakley

RG23

Pardown

RG25

M3

Junction 7

Grid references and labels:

- Farm
- Peter Houseman Rec. Grd.
- Manor House
- Oakley Jun. & Inf. Schs.
- Spinney Cott.
- Sewage Works
- Bull's Bushes Copse
- Bull's Bushes Farm
- Dean Heath Copse
- THE GREEN
- St. John's Copse
- Battledown Flyover Bri.
- Worting J.59tion
- Battledown Farm
- BATTLEDOWN COTTAGES
- Well's Copse
- Breach Farm
- Breach Cottages
- Leydown
- Jeffery's Copse
- Ply. Fld.
- Kings Orchard
- St. John's Piece
- Goddard's Firs
- Petersfield
- Water Ridges
- Small's Copse
- Pardown Copse
- Little Stubbs Copse
- South Wood
- Great Stubbs Copse
- Old Cottages
- Southwood Farm
- New Cottages
- Ganderdown Copse
- The Bungalow
- Ganderdown Cottages
- Kynance
- Oakdown Farm
- THE COPSE CARAVAN SITE
- Peak Copse
- Ind. Est.
- Subway
- WINCHESTER
- BASINGSTO
- DUMMER G
- WALTHAM ROAD
- NORTH WALTHAM ROAD
- RECTORY ROAD
- OAKLEY HILL ROAD
- WAYFARER'S WALK
- ST JOHNS ROAD
- PARDOWN LANE
- A30

Street names (East Oakley area): ARRAN, MULL, CAITHNESS, HIGHLAND, BRAEMAR, PARK, DR CROFT, AVIEMORE, CROFT, MARLBORO, LYTTON, TENNYSON, KENNET, NENE, MEDWAY, TAMAR, CL, ANTON, FROME, LYDE CL, MEON, HOOPERS LINK, MEDINA, BLACK, MATTHEWS WY, HOPPERS, STOUR GDNS, SEVERN GDNS, THE HALL, THE DRIVE, BEECH TREE LA, BARN, CEDAR TREE CL, ASH LA, OYSTER FRM RD, APPLE TREE CL, KINGS RD, ROYDEN, JOHN'S PIECE, MEAD, SAMPSON, LAURETIN DOWN

Column markers: A B C D E

Row markers: 1 2 3 4 5 6 7

Coordinate numbers: 57, 58, 59, 50, 49, 48, 47

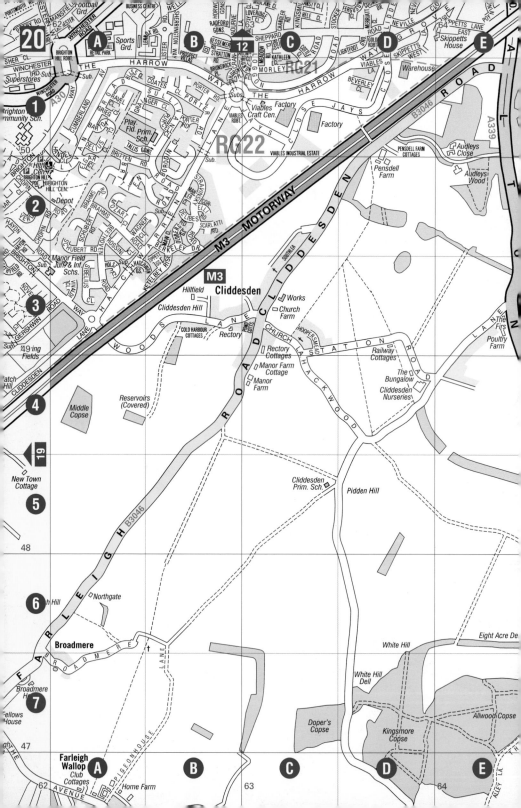

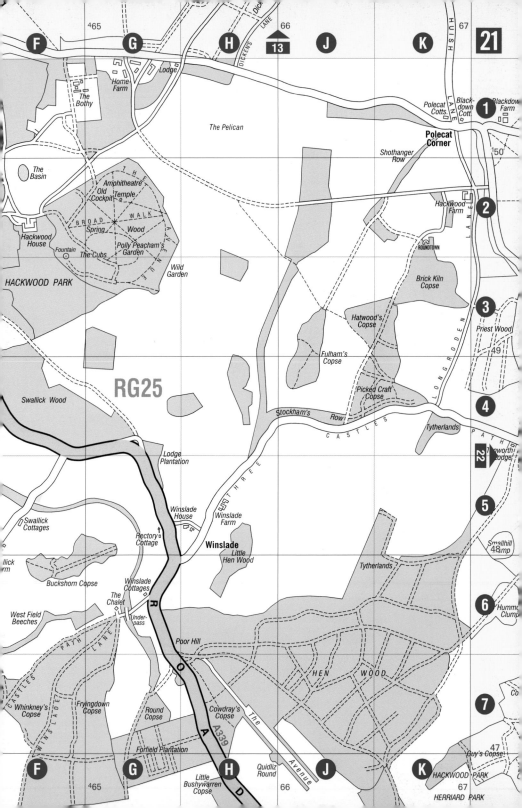

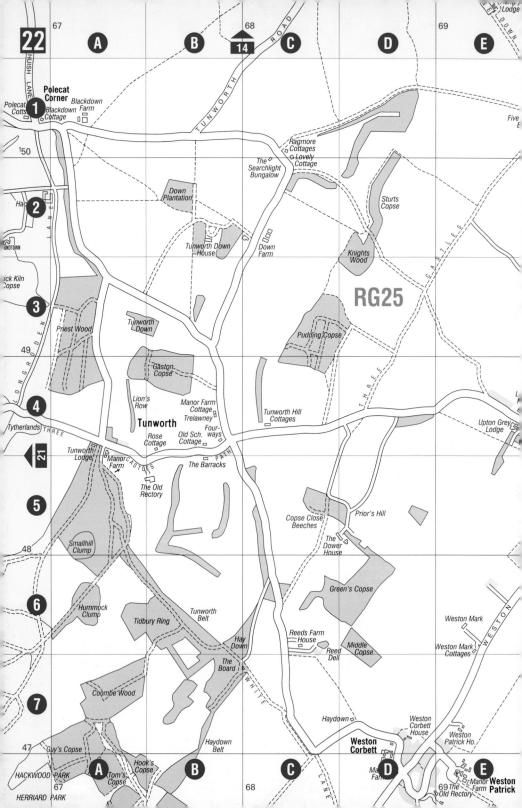

INDEX

Including Streets, Places & Areas, Hospitals & Hospices, Industrial Estates,
Selected Flats & Walkways and Selected Places of Interest.

HOW TO USE THIS INDEX

1. Each street name is followed by its Posttown or Postal Locality and then by its map reference; e.g. Abbey Rd. *B'stoke* . . . .7C **4** is in the Basingstoke Posttown and is to be found in square 7C on page **4**. The page number being shown in bold type.

2. A strict alphabetical order is followed in which Av., Rd., St., etc. (though abbreviated) are read in full and as part of the street name; e.g. Ash Gro. appears after Ashfield but before Ashlea.

3. Streets and a selection of flats and walkways too small to be shown on the maps, appear in the index in *Italics* with the thoroughfare to which it is connected shown in brackets; e.g. *Alexandra Ter. N War* . . . .*5C* **16** (off Bridge Rd.)

4. Places and areas are shown in the index in **blue type** and the map reference is to the actual map square in which the town centre or area is located and not to the place name shown on the map; e.g. **Andwell** **3E 14**

5. An example of a selected place of interest is Milestones Mus. 4A 12

6. An example of a hospital or hospice is HAMPSHIRE BMI CLINIC 3G 13

GENERAL ABBREVIATIONS

All : Alley	Ct : Court	Lit : Little	Rd : Road
App : Approach	Cres : Crescent	Lwr : Lower	Shop : Shopping
Arc : Arcade	Cft : Croft	Mc : Mac	S : South
Av : Avenue	Dri : Drive	Mnr : Manor	Sq : Square
Bk : Back	E : East	Mans : Mansions	Sta : Station
Boulevd : Boulevard	Embkmt : Embankment	Mkt : Market	St : Street
Bri : Bridge	Est : Estate	Mdw : Meadow	Ter : Terrace
B'way : Broadway	Fld : Field	M : Mews	Trad : Trading
Bldgs : Buildings	Gdns : Gardens	Mt : Mount	Up : Upper
Bus : Business	Gth : Garth	Mus : Museum	Va : Vale
Cvn : Caravan	Ga : Gate	N : North	Vw : View
Cen : Centre	Gt : Great	Pal : Palace	Vs : Villas
Chu : Church	Grn : Green	Pde : Parade	Vis : Visitors
Chyd : Churchyard	Gro : Grove	Pk : Park	Wlk : Walk
Circ : Circle	Ho : House	Pas : Passage	W : West
Cir : Circus	Ind : Industrial	Pl : Place	Yd : Yard
Clo : Close	Info : Information	Quad : Quadrant	
Comn : Common	Junct : Junction	Res : Residential	
Cotts : Cottages	La : Lane	Ri : Rise	

POSTTOWN AND POSTAL LOCALITY ABBREVIATIONS

And : Andwell	*H Wesp* : Hartley Wespall	*Nat S* : Nately Scures	*S Warn* : South Warnborough
B'stoke : Basingstoke	*H Wint* : Hartley Wintney	*Newn* : Newnham	*Tun* : Tunstall
Baug : Baughurst	*Hat W* : Hatch Warren	*N War* : North Warnborough	*Up Nat* : Up Nately
Brmly : Bramley	*Hook* : Hook	*Okly* : Oakley	*Up Wn* : Upper Wootton
Ch All : Charter Alley	*Hook C* : Hook Common	*Odi* : Odiham	*Upt G* : Upton Grey
Chine : Chineham	*Kemp* : Kempshott	*Old B* : Old Basing	*W'slde* : Winslade
Clid : Cliddesden	*Long S* : Long Sutton	*Ramsd* : Ramsdell	*Winch* : Winchfield
Dog : Dogmersfield	*Lych* : Lychpit	*Roth* : Rotherfield	*Woot L* : Wootton St Lawrence
Dum : Dummer	*Map* : Mapledurwell	*R'wick* : Rotherwick	*Wort* : Worting
Far W : Farleigh Wallop	*Matt* : Mattingley	*Sher J* : Sherborne St John	
Grey : Greywell	*Monk S* : Monk Sherborne	*Sher L* : Sherfield-on-Loddon	

A

Abbey Ct. *B'stoke* 7C **4**
Abbey Rd. *B'stoke* 7C **4**
Abbott Clo. *B'stoke* 7J **11**
Achilles Clo. *Chine* 4H **5**
Acorn Clo. *B'stoke* 4G **13**
Acton Ho. *B'stoke* 5A **12**
Adams Clo. *N War* 6B **16**
Addison Gdns. *Odi* 6E **16**
Adrian Clo. *H Wint* 3K **9**
Aghemund Clo. *Chine* 5G **5**
Ajax Clo. *Chine* 4H **5**
Alanbrooke Clo.
   H Wint 2J **9**
Albert Yd. *B'stoke* 5D **12**
Albion Pl. *H Wint* 2J **9**
Aldermaston Rd.
   Monk S 1K **3**
Aldermaston Rd.
   Sher J & B'stoke 5K **3**
Aldermaston Rd. Roundabout.
   B'stoke 1B **12**

Aldermaston Rd. S.
   B'stoke 2B **12**
Alderney Av. *B'stoke* 3H **19**
Alders Clo. *B'stoke* 4F **13**
Alderwood. *Chine* 5H **5**
Alderwood Dri. *Hook* 6B **8**
Aldworth Cres. *B'stoke* 5A **12**
Alencon Link. *B'stoke* 4C **12**
Alexandra Rd. *B'stoke* 4B **12**
Alexandra Ter. N War 5C **16**
   (off Bridge Rd.)
Allen Clo. *B'stoke* 6B **12**
Allenmoor La. *Roth* 1J **7**
Alley La. *W'slde* 7E **20**
Alliston Way. *B'stoke* 6H **11**
Allnutt Av. *B'stoke* 4E **12**
Almond Clo. *Old B* 3J **13**
Alpine Ct. *B'stoke* 6G **11**
Alton Rd. *S Warn* 7A **24**
Alton Rd. *B'stoke & W'slde*
   . . . . .1E **20**
Amazon Clo. *B'stoke* 5B **12**
Amport Clo. *Lych* 1J **13**
Anchor Yd. *B'stoke* 5D **12**

Andover Rd. *Okly* 6A **10**
Andrew Clo. *N War* 6B **16**
Andwell. **3E 14**
Andwell Drove.
   And & Map 4E **14**
Andwell La. *And* 4E **14**
Angel Meadows. *Odi* 6E **16**
Anglers Pl. *B'stoke* 4F **13**
Anglesey Clo. *B'stoke* 6E **4**
Anstey Clo. *B'stoke* 7C **12**
Antar Clo. *B'stoke* 5B **12**
Anton Clo. *Okly* 1B **18**
Antrim Clo. *B'stoke* 6H **11**
Applegarth Clo. *B'stoke* 6E **12**
Appletree Clo. *Okly* 2B **18**
Appletree Mead. *Hook* 7C **8**
Apple Way. *Old B* 4K **13**
Arcadia Clo. *Hat W* 6G **19**
Archery Fields. *Odi* 6F **17**
Arlott Dri. *B'stoke* 2D **12**
Armstrong Rd. *B'stoke* 2G **13**
Arne Clo. *B'stoke* 3K **19**
Arran Clo. *Okly* 7A **10**

Arrow La. *H Wint* 2H **9**
Arun Ct. *B'stoke* 4F **13**
Arundel Gdns. *B'stoke* 2J **15**
Ascension Clo. *B'stoke* 7F **5**
Ashe Clo. *Woot L* 2F **11**
Ashfield. *Chine* 5H **5**
Ash Gro. *Old B* 3A **14**
Ashlea. *Hook* 6B **8**
Ashley Lodge. *B'stoke* 6C **12**
   (off Frescade Cres.)
Ashmoor La. *Old B* 3B **14**
Ash Tree Clo. *Okly* 2A **18**
Ashwood. *Chine* 6G **5**
Ashwood Way. *B'stoke* 2K **11**
Ashwood Way Roundabout.
   B'stoke 2K **11**
Aspen Gdns. *Hook* 6B **8**
Aster Rd. *B'stoke* 3G **19**
Attwood Clo. *B'stoke* 5B **12**
Attwood Clo. Mobile Home Pk.
   B'stoke 5B **12**
Augustus Dri. *B'stoke* 2J **11**
Auklet Clo. *B'stoke* 3F **19**
Austen Gro. *B'stoke* 7A **12**

Anvil Theatre. 4D **12**

Avenue, The—Churchill Av.

Avenue, The. *Far W* 7K 19
Avenue, The. *B'stoke* 2G 21
Aviary Ct. *B'stoke* 1G 13
Aviemore Dri. *Okly* 1A 18
Avon Rd. *Okly* 1B 18
Avon Wlk. *B'stoke* 4F 13
Ayliffe Ho. *B'stoke* 5K 11
Aylings Clo. *B'stoke* 4H 11
Aylwin Clo. *B'stoke* 7C 12

B

Bach Clo. *B'stoke* 3K 19
Badgers Bank. *Lych* 1H 13
Bagwell La. *Odi & Winch* 4G 17
Baird Av. *B'stoke* 7A 12
Ballard Clo. *B'stoke* 6J 11
Balmoral Ct. *B'stoke* 6J 11
Balmoral Way. *B'stoke* 4G 19
Balsan Clo. *B'stoke* 1K 11
Band Hall Pl. *Hook* 7B 8
Barbel Av. *B'stoke* 4G 13
Barbour Clo. *Odi* 2C 24
Bardwell Clo. *B'stoke* 5J 11
Baredown, The. *Nat S* 2H 15
Barn La. *Okly* 2A 18
Barnwells Ct. *H Wint* 1K 9
Barra Clo. *Okly* 7A 10
Barrett Ct. *B'stoke* 7E 12
Barron Pl. *B'stoke* 1H 11
Barry Way. *B'stoke* 3K 19
Bartley Way. *Hook* 1C 16
Bartley Wood Bus. Pk. E. *Hook* 1C 16
Bartley Wood Bus. Pk. W. *Hook* 1B 16
Bartok Clo. *B'stoke* 1A 20
Barton's Ct. *Odi* 6D 16
Barton's La. *Old B* 2H 13 (in three parts)
Basingfield Clo. *Old B* 5K 13
Basing House. 3J 13
Basing Rd. *Old B* 3G 13
Basingstoke. 4B 12
Basingstoke Bus. Cen. *B'stoke* 7A 12
Basingstoke Cricket Club. 5C 12
Basingstoke Enterprise Cen. *B'stoke* 5H 11
Basingstoke Golf Club. 5F 19
Basingstoke Ice Rink. 4J 11
Basingstoke Rd. *Ramsd* 1E 2
Basing Vw. *B'stoke* 4E 12
Batchelor Dri. *Old B* 4A 14
Battledown Cotts. *Okly* 1E 18
Baughurst Rd. *Ramsd* 1D 2
Baynard Clo. *B'stoke* 2E 12
Beach Piece Way. *B'stoke* 3H 19
Beaconsfield Rd. *B'stoke* 5D 12
Beal's Pightle. *Ch All* 1F 3
Bear Ct. *B'stoke* 2H 13
Beauclerk Grn. *Winch* 7J 9
Beaulieu Ct. B'stoke 4F 13 *(off Loddon Dri.)*
Beckett Clo. *B'stoke* 4G 11
Beckett Ct. *Wort* 5G 11
Beddington Ct. *Lych* 1J 13
Bedford Wlk. B'stoke 4D 12 *(off Festival Pl.)*
Beecham Berry. *B'stoke* 3K 19
Beechcrest Vw. *Hook* 6B 8
Beechdown Ho. *B'stoke* 1J 19
Beech Dri. *Chine* 5J 5
Beeches, The. *Hat W* 4J 19
Beech Tree Clo. *Okly* 2A 18
Beech Way. *B'stoke* 2J 11
Beechwood. *Chine* 5G 5
Beechwood Clo. *B'stoke* 4J 19
Beethoven Rd. *B'stoke* 2A 20
Begonia Clo. *B'stoke* 3G 19
Belfry Sq. *Hat W* 5G 19
Belgrave M. *H Wint* 2K 9
Belle Vue Rd. *Old B* 3K 13
Bell Mdw. Rd. *Hook* 7B 8
Bell Rd. *B'stoke* 2G 13
Belmont Heights. *Hat W* 5J 19
Belvedere Gdns. *Chine* 4J 5
Benford Ct. Odi 7E 16 *(off Buryfields)*
Bennet Clo. *B'stoke* 2E 12
Benwell Clo. *Odi* 2C 24
Beresford Cen., The. *B'stoke* 1G 13
Berewyk Clo. *B'stoke* 3G 19
Berkeley Dri. *B'stoke* 2B 20
Berk Ho. *B'stoke* 3F 13
Bermuda Clo. *B'stoke* 6E 4
Bernstein Rd. *B'stoke* 3J 19
Berry Ct. *Hook* 1A 16
Berwyn Clo. *B'stoke* 6G 11
Bessemer Rd. *B'stoke* 7B 12
Beverley Clo. *B'stoke* 1D 20
Bexmoor. *Old B* 3J 13
Bexmoor Way. *Old B* 3J 13
Bidden. 3H 23
Bidden Rd. *Upt G & N War* 5F 23
Bilton Ind. Est. *B'stoke* 7G 5
Bilton Rd. *B'stoke* 7G 5
Binfields Clo. *Chine* 7H 5
Binfields Farm La. *Chine* 7H 5
Binfields Roundabout. *Lych* 6H 5
Bingley Clo. *B'stoke* 2E 12
Birches Crest. *Hat W* 4K 19
Birch Gro. *Hook* 6B 8
Birchwood. *Chine* 5H 5
Bittern Clo. *B'stoke* 2F 19
Blackberry Wlk. *Lych* 2G 13
Blackbird Clo. *B'stoke* 2F 19
Black Dam. 6F 13
Black Dam Cen. *B'stoke* 6F 13
Blackdam Nature Reserve. 5H 13
Black Dam Roundabout. *B'stoke* 5G 13
Black Dam Way. *B'stoke* 6F 13
Blackdown Clo. *B'stoke* 6H 11
Blackstocks La. *Nat S* 4F 15
Blackthorn Way. *B'stoke* 3J 11
Blackwater Clo. *Okly* 1B 18
Blackwater Clo. *B'stoke* 4E 12
Blaegrove La. *Up Nat* 5F 15
Blair Rd. *B'stoke* 6C 12
Blake Clo. *Odi* 2C 24
Blenheim Rd. *Old B* 4A 14
Bliss Clo. *B'stoke* 1A 20
Bluehaven Wlk. *Hook* 7K 7
Blunden Clo. *B'stoke* 1C 20
Bodmin Clo. *B'stoke* 6H 11
Bolton Cres. *B'stoke* 6A 12
Bond Clo. *B'stoke* 1G 13
Boon Way. *Okly* 7A 10
Borodin Clo. *B'stoke* 2B 20
Borough Ct. Rd. *H Wint* 5E 8
Bottle La. *Matt* 1B 8
Bounty Ri. *B'stoke* 5C 12
Bounty Rd. *B'stoke* 5C 12
Bourne Ct. *B'stoke* 4F 13
Bourne Fld. *Sher J* 4A 4
Bow Fld. *Hook* 7C 8
Bowling Grn. Dri. *Hook* 7K 7
Bowman Rd. *Chine* 4H 5
Bowyer Clo. *B'stoke* 5C 12
Boyce Clo. *B'stoke* 2J 19
Bracken Bank. *Lych* 1H 13
Brackens, The. *B'stoke* 4J 19
Brackley Av. *H Wint* 2H 9
Brackley Way. *B'stoke* 1J 19
Bracknell La. *H Wint* 1H 9
Braemar Dri. *Okly* 7A 10
Brahms Rd. *B'stoke* 2A 20
Braine L'Alleud Rd. *B'stoke* 3D 12
Bramble Way. *Old B* 3A 14
Brambling Clo. *B'stoke* 3F 19
Bramblys Clo. *B'stoke* 5C 12
Bramblys Dri. *B'stoke* 5C 12
Bramdown Heights. *B'stoke* 4H 19
Bramley Rd. *Brmly* 1E 4
Brampton Gdns. *Hat W* 5J 19
Bramshott Dri. *Hook* 7B 8
Branton Clo. *B'stoke* 6J 11
Breadels Fld. *Hat W* 6G 19
Brewer Clo. *B'stoke* 6J 11
Brewhouse La. *H Wint* 2K 9
Brickfields Clo. *Lych* 1H 13
Bridge Rd. *N War* 5C 16
Brighton Hill. 2J 19
Brighton Hill Cen. *B'stoke* 2K 19
Brighton Hill Pde. *B'stoke* 2K 19
Brighton Hill Retail Pk. *B'stoke* 7A 12
Brighton Hill Roundabout. *B'stoke* 7A 12
Brighton Way. *B'stoke* 2K 19
Britannia Dri. *Hat W* 6G 19
Britten Rd. *B'stoke* 1A 20
Broadhurst Gro. *Lych* 2H 13
Broad Leaze. *Hook* 6A 8
Broadmere. 6A 20
Broadmere. *Far W* 7A 20
Broad Oak. 5G 17
Broad Oak La. *Odi* 6G 17
Broad Wlk. *B'stoke* 2G 21
Brocas Dri. *B'stoke* 2E 12
Bronze Clo. *Hat W* 6G 19
Brookfield Clo. *Chine* 5J 5
Brookvale Clo. *B'stoke* 4C 12
Brown Cft. *Hook* 7K 7
Browning Clo. *B'stoke* 1E 12
Brunel Rd. *B'stoke* 3A 12
Brunswick Pl. *B'stoke* 1B 20
Buckby La. *B'stoke* 4F 13
Buckfast Clo. *B'stoke* 7C 4
Buckingham Ct. *B'stoke* 2G 19
Buckingham Pde. *B'stoke* 1G 19
Buckland Av. *B'stoke* 1K 19
Buckland Pde. *B'stoke* 7K 11
Buckskin. 6J 11
Buckskin La. *B'stoke* 7G 11
Budd's Clo. *B'stoke* 5C 12
Buffins Corner. *Odi* 7C 16
Buffins Rd. *Odi* 7C 16
Bunnian Pl. *B'stoke* 3D 12
Bunting M. *B'stoke* 3F 19
Burgess Clo. *Odi* 7C 16
Burgess Rd. *B'stoke* 3C 12
Burnaby Clo. *B'stoke* 6J 11
Burns Clo. *B'stoke* 1E 12
Burrowfields. *B'stoke* 5H 19
Burton's Gdns. *Old B* 2K 13
Buryfields. *Odi* 7E 16
Bury Rd. *B'stoke* 3K 11
Bury, The. 7E 16
Bury, The. *Odi* 6E 16
Butler Clo. *B'stoke* 5J 11
Buttermere Dri. *B'stoke* 1G 19
Butts Mdw. *Hook* 7A 8
Butty, The. *B'stoke* 4F 13
Byfleet Av. *Old B* 3K 13
Byrd Gdns. *B'stoke* 3J 19
Byron Clo. *B'stoke* 7F 5

C

Cadnam Clo. *Okly* 7B 10
Caernarvon Clo. *B'stoke* 4J 11
Caesar Clo. *B'stoke* 2J 11
Cairngorm Clo. *B'stoke* 5H 11
Caithness Clo. *Okly* 1A 18
Calleva Clo. *B'stoke* 3H 19
Camberry Clo. *B'stoke* 6E 12
Cambrian Way. *B'stoke* 6H 11
Camfield Clo. *B'stoke* 6E 12
Camford Clo. *B'stoke* 6G 19
Camlea Clo. *B'stoke* 6E 12
Campion Way. *H Wint* 1K 9
Campsie Clo. *B'stoke* 5H 11
Camrose Way. *B'stoke* 7E 12
Cam Wlk. *B'stoke* 4F 13
Camwood Clo. *B'stoke* 6E 12
Canal Clo. *N War* 5C 16
Canberra Way. *Hat W* 6G 19
Cannock Ct. *B'stoke* 5J 11
Canterbury Clo. *B'stoke* 2H 19
Carbonel Clo. *B'stoke* 4G 11
Carisbrooke Clo. *B'stoke* 3J 11
Carleton Clo. *Hook* 7K 7
Carlisle Clo. *B'stoke* 3J 11
Carmichael Way. *B'stoke* 2J 19
Carpenters Ct. *B'stoke* 7K 11
Carpenter's Down. *B'stoke* 7D 4
Cartel Units. *B'stoke* 1G 13
Castle Ri. *N War* 5C 16
Castle Rd. *B'stoke* 6D 12
Castle Sq. *B'stoke* 4D 12
Caston's Wlk. *B'stoke* 5D 12
Caston's Yd. *B'stoke* 5D 12
Catkin Clo. *Chine* 5H 5
Causeway Cotts. *H Wint* 2K 9
Cavalier Clo. *Old B* 3A 14
Cavalier Rd. *Old B* 3A 14
Cavel Ct. *B'stoke* 1J 13
Cayman Clo. *B'stoke* 7F 5
Cedar Ter. *H Wint* 3H 9
Cedar Tree Clo. *Okly* 2A 18
Cedar Way. *B'stoke* 2K 11
Cedarwood. *Chine* 5F 5
Cemetery Hill. *Odi* 7E 16
Centre Dri. *Chine* 7H 5
Centurion Way. *B'stoke* 3H 19 (in two parts)
Chaffers Clo. *Long S* 7D 24
Chaffinch Clo. *B'stoke* 2G 19
Chaldon Grn. *Lych* 1J 13
Chalk Va. *Old B* 4A 14
Chalky Copse. *Hook* 6A 8
Chalky La. *Dog* 7K 17
Challis Clo. *B'stoke* 7J 11
Challoner Clo. *B'stoke* 6J 11
Chandler Rd. *B'stoke* 7C 12
Chantry Clo. *Hook* 1A 16
Chantry M. *B'stoke* 3H 19
Chapel Clo. *Old B* 2K 13
Chapel Hill. *B'stoke* 3C 12
Chapel Pond Dri. *N War* 6C 16
Chapel Row. *H Wint* 1K 9
Chapter Ter. *H Wint* 1K 9
Charles Clo. *Hook* 7A 8
Charles Richards Clo. *B'stoke* 6C 12
Charles St. *B'stoke* 5K 11
Charnwood Clo. *B'stoke* 6H 11
Charter Alley. 1F 3
Chatsworth Grn. *Hat W* 4J 19
Chaucer Clo. *B'stoke* 7E 4
Chelmer Ct. B'stoke 4F 13 *(off Loddon Dri.)*
Chelsea Ho. B'stoke 4D 12 *(off Festival Pl.)*
Chequers Rd. *B'stoke* 4E 12
Cherry Clo. *Hook* 6B 8
Cherry Tree Wlk. *B'stoke* 1E 12
Cherrywood. *Chine* 5G 5
Chesterfield Rd. *B'stoke* 6E 12
Chester Pl. *B'stoke* 5C 12
Chestnut Bank. *Old B* 2K 13
Cheviot Clo. *B'stoke* 6H 11
Chichester Pl. *B'stoke* 7A 12
Chiltern Way. *B'stoke* 6G 11
Chilton Ridge. *Hat W* 5H 19
Chineham. 6H 5
Chineham Bus. Pk. *Chine* 4G 5
Chineham District Cen. *Chine* 7H 5
Chineham La. *B'stoke* 1E 12
Chineham La. *Sher J* 6B 4
Chineham Pk. Ct. *B'stoke* 1F 13
Chivers Clo. *B'stoke* 6H 11
Chopin Rd. *B'stoke* 2K 19
Church End. 2A 6
Churchill Av. *Odi* 1D 24

26 A-Z Basingstoke

George St.—Lampards Clo.

George St. B'stoke 4B 12
Gershwin Ct. B'stoke 2K 19
Gershwin Rd. B'stoke 2J 19
Gilbard Ct. Chine 5J 5
Gilbert Clo. B'stoke 7E 4
Gillies Dri. B'stoke 1J 11
Glade Clo. Chine 6H 5
Glamis Clo. Okly 7B 10
Glastonbury Clo. B'stoke 1C 12
Glebe La. Wort 5G 11
Glebe La. H Wint 3K 9
Gleneagles Clo. Hat W 5G 19
Gloucester Dri. B'stoke 2H 19
Goat La. B'stoke 4E 12
Goddards Firs. Okly 2C 18
Goddards La. Sher L 1A 6
Golden Lion Roundabout. B'stoke 7D 12
Goldfinch Gdns. B'stoke 4F 19
Goodman Clo. B'stoke 5B 12
Goose Grn. Hook 6K 7
Goose La. Hook 6A 8
Gordon Clo. B'stoke 3E 12
Gower Clo. B'stoke 2D 12
Gower Cres. Hook 7B 8
Gracemere Cres. B'stoke 3F 19
Grafton Way. B'stoke 5K 11
Grainger Clo. B'stoke 1A 20
Grampian Way. B'stoke 6H 11
Grange La. H Wint 2H 9
Gt. Binfields Cres. Lych 1H 13
Gt. Binfields Rd. Lych 7H 5
Gt. Oaks Chase. Chine 6G 5
Gt. Sheldons Coppice. Hook 7K 7
Gt. Western Cotts. B'stoke 3D 12
Grebe Clo. B'stoke 3F 19
Greenaways, The. Okly 7B 10
Greenbirch Clo. B'stoke 3F 19
Greenbury Clo. B'stoke 4J 11
Green La. H Wint 3J 9
Green La. R'wick 4J 7
Green, The. N War 4B 16
Green Way. B'stoke 4J 11 (in two parts)
Greenwood Dri. Chine 4H 5
Gregory Clo. B'stoke 2E 12
Gregory Ho. Hook 7A 8
Gresley Rd. B'stoke 3E 12
Greywell. 7K 15
Greywell Rd. Map & Upt G 4B 14
Greywell Rd. Up Nat 4F 15
Grieg Clo. B'stoke 1A 20
Griffin Way N. Hook 5B 8
Griffin Way S. Hook 6C 8
Grosvenor Clo. Hat W 5H 19
Grosvenor Ho. B'stoke 4E 12
Grove Clo. B'stoke 6E 12
Grove Rd. B'stoke 7D 12
Guernsey Clo. B'stoke 6E 4
Guinea Ct. Chine 4J 5
Gurney Ct. Odi 7D 16

H

Hackwood Cotts. B'stoke 7E 12
Hackwood La. Clid 4C 20
Hackwood Rd. B'stoke 5D 12
Hackwood Rd. Roundabout. B'stoke 6E 12
Hadleigh Pl. B'stoke 4C 12
Hadrians Way. B'stoke 2J 11
Hailstone Rd. B'stoke 1D 12
Halliday Clo. B'stoke 7C 12
Halls La. Roth 1J 7
Hamble Clo. Okly 1B 18
Hamble Ct. B'stoke 4F 13
Hamelyn Clo. B'stoke 5C 12
Hamelyn Rd. B'stoke 5C 12
Hamilton Clo. B'stoke 2A 12
Hammond Rd. B'stoke 6C 12
HAMPSHIRE BMI CLINIC. 3G 13
Hampshire Clo. B'stoke 6G 11
Hampshire International Bus. Pk. Chine 4G 5
Hampstead Ho. B'stoke 4D 12 (off Church St.)
Hampton Ct. B'stoke 3K 11
Handel Clo. B'stoke 1A 20
Hanmore Rd. Chine 6G 5
Hanover Gdns. B'stoke 7C 12
Hardings La. H Wint 2K 9
Hardy La. B'stoke 5C 12
Harebell Clo. H Wint 1K 9
Harebell Gdns. H Wint 1K 9
Hare's La. H Wint 1K 9
Harfield Clo. Hook 7A 8
Harlech Clo. B'stoke 4J 11
Harold Jackson Ter. B'stoke 5E 12
Harris Hill. B'stoke 3H 19
Harrow Way, The. B'stoke 1A 20
Hartford Ct. H Wint 2K 9
Hartford Rd. H Wint 2J 9
Hartford Ter. H Wint 2K 9
Hartley M. H Wint 1K 9 (off High St.)
Hartley Wintney. 2J 9
Hartley Wintney Golf Course. 1K 9
Hartswood. Chine 6G 5
Harvest Way. Lych 2H 13
Hassocks Workshops. B'stoke 2G 13
Hastings Clo. B'stoke 4H 11
Hatch. 4B 14
Hatch Cvn. Pk. Old B 5A 14
Hatch La. Old B 3K 13
Hatch Warren. 4H 19
Hatch Warren Cotts. Hat W 3J 19
Hatchwarren Gdns. B'stoke 3A 20
Hatch Warren La. B'stoke & Hat W 3H 19 (in three parts)
Hatchwarren La. B'stoke 3A 20
Hatch Warren Retail Pk. B'stoke 4G 19
Hathaway Gdns. B'stoke 1F 13
Hawk Clo. B'stoke 2F 19
Hawkes Clo. H Wint 1J 9
Hawkfield La. B'stoke 5C 12
Hawthorn Ri. Hook 6B 8
Hawthorn Way. B'stoke 3J 11
Haydn Rd. B'stoke 2K 19
Hayley La. Long S 5B 24
Haymarket Theatre. 5D 12
Haywarden Pl. H Wint 1K 9
Hazel Clo. Okly 1B 18
Hazel Coppice. Hook 6B 8
Hazeldene. Chine 6H 5
Hazeley Bottom. 1G 9
Hazeley Clo. H Wint 1J 9
Hazelwood. Chine 4G 5
Hazelwood Clo. B'stoke 2K 11
Hazelwood Dri. B'stoke 2K 11
Headington Clo. B'stoke 2K 19
Heather Gro. H Wint 1J 9
Heather La. Up Nat 4G 15
Heather Row La. Nat S 2J 15
Heather Row La. Up Nat & Nat S 5G 15
Heather Way. Kemp 3G 19
Heathfield Rd. B'stoke 3K 19
Heathside Way. H Wint 1J 9
Heathview. Hook 6C 8
Hedgerows, The. Lych 1J 13
Hele Clo. B'stoke 7C 12
Hepplewhite Dri. B'stoke 3G 19
Hereford Clo. Odi 7C 16
Hereford Rd. B'stoke 4J 11
Heritage Pk. B'stoke 5H 19
Heritage Vw. Hat W 5H 19
Heron Pk. Lych 7H 5
Heron Way. B'stoke 2F 19
Hesters Vw. Long S 7D 24
Highdowns. Hat W 4J 19
High Dri. B'stoke 7J 11
Higher Mead. Lych 1H 13
Highfield Chase. B'stoke 4B 12
Highland Dri. Okly 7A 10
Highlands Rd. B'stoke 6G 11
Highmoors. Chine 5H 5
Highpath Way. B'stoke 1J 11
High St. H Wint 2K 9
High St. Odi 6D 16
Highwood Ridge. B'stoke 4H 19
Hillary Rd. B'stoke 2B 12
Hillcrest Ct. B'stoke 3H 11
Hillcrest Wlk. B'stoke 4H 11
Hill Rd. Okly 1A 18
Hill Side. 7G 17
Hillside Rd. Odi 1E 24
Hill Sq. Lych 7J 5
Hillstead Ct. B'stoke 5D 12
Hill Vw. Rd. B'stoke 6A 12
Hogarth Clo. B'stoke 5G 13
Holbein Clo. B'stoke 6F 13
Hollin's Wlk. B'stoke 4D 12 (off Festival Pl.)
Holly Dri. Old B 3A 14
Hollyhock Clo. B'stoke 2G 19
Holmes Clo. B'stoke 4J 19
Holst Clo. B'stoke 3A 20
Holt La. Hook 2C 16
Holt Way. Hook 6C 8
Holy Barn Clo. B'stoke 1G 19
Holyrood Ct. B'stoke 6H 11
Homefield Way. B'stoke 7J 3
Homesteads Rd. B'stoke 1G 19
Honeysuckle Clo. B'stoke 2G 19
Hook. 7B 8
Hook Common. 2K 15
Hook La. Okly & Up Wn 2A 10
Hook Rd. Grey & N War 5K 15
Hook Rd. Hook 2A 16
Hook Rd. N War 4C 16
Hook Rd. R'wick 3K 7
Hoopersmead. Clid 3C 20
Hoopers Way. Okly 1B 18
Hopfield Rd. H Wint 3J 9
Hop Garden Rd. Hook 7K 7
Hopton Gth. Lych 7J 5
Hornbeam Pl. Hook 6B 8
Horwood Gdns. B'stoke 7B 12
Houndmills. 3A 12
Houndmills Rd. B'stoke 3A 12
Houndmills Roundabout. B'stoke 2B 12
Howard Rd. B'stoke 6E 12
Howard Vw. B'stoke 6K 11
Hubbard Rd. B'stoke 2B 12
Huish La. Old B 5K 13
Hulbert Way. B'stoke 7J 11
Hunters Clo. Okly 6B 10
Hunts Clo. Hook 7C 8
Hunts Comn. H Wint 1K 9
Hunts Cotts. H Wint 1K 9
Hurne Ct. B'stoke 4F 13 (off Lytton Rd.)
Hyacinth Clo. B'stoke 2G 19
Hyde Rd. Long S 7E 24

I

Inglewood Dri. B'stoke 4H 19
Inkpen Gdns. Lych 1J 13
Intec Bus. Cen. B'stoke 1G 13
Iris Clo. B'stoke 3G 19
Irwell Clo. B'stoke 4F 13
Itchen Clo. Okly 1B 18
Ivar Gdns. Lych 1J 13

J

Jackdaw Clo. B'stoke 2F 19
Jacob's All. B'stoke 5D 12
Jacob's Yd. B'stoke 5D 12
James Clo. B'stoke 2E 12
Jasmine Rd. B'stoke 2H 19
Jays Clo. B'stoke 1C 20
Jefferson Rd. B'stoke 2D 12
Jersey Clo. B'stoke 6E 4
John Eddie Ct. B'stoke 6J 11
John Morgan Clo. Hook 6A 8
Joices Yd. B'stoke 5D 12
Joule Rd. B'stoke 2B 12
Jubilee Rd. B'stoke 5D 12
Julius Clo. B'stoke 1J 11
June Dri. B'stoke 4H 11
Juniper Clo. Chine 4J 5

K

Kathleen Clo. B'stoke 7C 12
Keats Clo. B'stoke 7E 4
Kelvin Hill. B'stoke 6A 12
Kembers La. Map 5C 14
Kempshott. 2H 19
Kempshott Gdns. B'stoke 2G 19
Kempshott Gro. B'stoke 5G 11
Kempshott La. B'stoke 3G 19
Kempshott Pk. Ind. Est. Kemp 7F 19
Kempshott Roundabout. Kemp 3H 19
Kendal Gdns. B'stoke 7H 11
Kenilworth Rd. B'stoke 3H 11
Kennet Clo. B'stoke 4F 13
Kennet Way. Okly 1B 18
Kensington Ho. B'stoke 4D 12 (off Festival Pl.)
Kerfield Way. Hook 7B 8
Kersley Cres. Odi 2C 24
Kestrel Rd. B'stoke 1F 19
Ketelbey Ri. B'stoke 3B 20
Keytech Cen. B'stoke 2K 11
Kiln Gdns. H Wint 2J 9
Kiln La. Monk S 3G 3
Kiln Rd. Sher J 5A 4
Kimbell Rd. B'stoke 7B 12
Kimber Clo. Chine 6H 5
Kimberley Rd. B'stoke 6A 12
Kingfisher Clo. B'stoke 1F 19
Kingfisher Ct. B'stoke 3C 12
King Johns Rd. N War 5C 16
Kingsbridge Copse. Newn 1J 15
Kingsclere Rd. B'stoke 2B 12
Kingsclere Rd. Ramsd & B'stoke 4A 2 (in two parts)
King's Furlong. 6C 12
Kings Furlong Cen. B'stoke 6C 12
King's Furlong Dri. B'stoke 6B 12
Kingsland Ind. Pk. B'stoke 7G 5
Kingsmill Rd. B'stoke 7C 12
Kings Orchard. Okly 2B 18
Kings Pightle. Chine 5H 5
King's Rd. B'stoke 6A 12
King St. Odi 6E 16 (in two parts)
Kingsvale Ct. B'stoke 5B 12
Kintyre Clo. Okly 7A 10
Kipling Wlk. B'stoke 6A 12
Kite Hill Cotts. B'stoke 6G 11
Knights Pk. B'stoke 2B 12
Knights Pk. Rd. B'stoke 2B 12
Knight St. B'stoke 5B 12

L

Laburnum Way. B'stoke 3K 11
Laffans Rd. Odi 1D 24
Lake Vw. H Wint 1K 9
Lambs Row. Lych 2H 13
Lampards Clo. R'wick 2K 7

28 A-Z Basingstoke

Lancaster Rd. *B'stoke* ...3C **12**
Landseer Clo. *B'stoke* ...6F **13**
Lansley Rd. *B'stoke* ...1D **12**
Lapin La. *B'stoke* ...5H **19**
Larchwood. *Chine* ...4F **5**
(Crockford La.)
Larchwood. *Chine* ...5H **5**
(Hanmore Rd.)
Lark Clo. *B'stoke* ...2F **19**
Larkfield. *Chine* ...5H **5**
Laurel Clo. *N War* ...6C **16**
Laurels, The. *B'stoke* ...3E **12**
Lavender Rd. *B'stoke* ...3G **19**
Lavington Cotts. *B'stoke* ...1K **13**
Lawrence Clo. *B'stoke* ...7E **4**
Lawrencedale Ct. *B'stoke* ...5B **12**
Lay Fld. *Hook* ...7K **7**
Lea Clo. *B'stoke* ...4F **13**
Leaden Vere. *Long S* ...6D **24**
Lees Hill. *S Warn* ...6J **23**
Lees Mdw. *Hook* ...7C **8**
Lefroy Av. *B'stoke* ...2E **12**
Lefroy Ho. *B'stoke* ...2E **12**
Lehar Clo. *B'stoke* ...2K **19**
Lennon Way. *B'stoke* ...2J **19**
Lennox Rd. *B'stoke* ...7B **12**
Len Smart Ct. *B'stoke* ...2E **12**
Lewis Clo. *B'stoke* ...2E **12**
Lightfoot Gro. *B'stoke* ...7D **12**
Lightsfield. *Okly* ...7B **10**
Lilac Way. *B'stoke* ...3K **11**
Lily Clo. *B'stoke* ...2G **19**
Lime Gdns. *B'stoke* ...4F **13**
Limes, The. *B'stoke* ...2G **19**
Lime Tree Way. *Chine* ...5G **5**
Lincoln Clo. *B'stoke* ...3H **19**
Linden Av. *Old B* ...4K **13**
Linden Av. *Odi* ...5F **17**
Linden Ct. *Old B* ...4K **13**
Lingfield Clo. *Old B* ...4A **14**
Link Way. *Okly* ...1B **18**
Linnet Clo. *B'stoke* ...7G **11**
Lion Ct. *B'stoke* ...3H **13**
Lisa Ct. *B'stoke* ...5C **12**
Lister Rd. *B'stoke* ...7B **12**
Little Basing. *Old B* ...2H **13**
Lit. Binfields. *Chine* ...7J **5**
Lit. Copse Chase. *Chine* ...6G **5**
Lit. Dean La. *Upt G* ...6H **23**
Little Fallow. *Lych* ...1H **13**
Lit. Hoddington. *Upt G* ...5G **23**
Lit. Hoddington Clo.
Upt G ...5G **23**
Litton Gdns. *Okly* ...1B **18**
Locksmead. *B'stoke* ...4F **13**
Loddon Bus. Cen. *B'stoke* ...2G **13**
Loddon Cen., The. *B'stoke* ...1G **13**
Loddon Ct. *B'stoke* ...7D **12**
Loddon Dri. *B'stoke* ...4E **12**
Loddon Ho. *B'stoke* ...3E **12**
Loddon Mall. *B'stoke* ...4D **12**
Loggon Rd. *B'stoke* ...7C **12**
Lomond Clo. *Okly* ...7A **10**
London Rd. *And & H Wint* ...3D **14**
London Rd. *Old B* ...5G **13**
London Rd. *B'stoke* ...5E **12**
London Rd. *H Wint* ...1K **9**
London Rd. *Hook & H Wint* ...6C **8**
London Rd. *Odi* ...6E **16**
(in two parts)
London St. *B'stoke* ...5D **12**
Longacre Ri. *Chine* ...6G **5**
Long Copse Chase.
Chine ...6G **5**
Longcroft Clo. *B'stoke* ...5C **12**
Long Cross La. *Hat W* ...4G **19**
Longfellow Pde. *B'stoke* ...1E **12**
Longfield. *Okly* ...6B **10**
Long La. *Chine* ...6J **5**
Long La. *Odi* ...1E **24**
Longmoor Rd. *B'stoke* ...5C **12**
Longroden La. *Tun* ...4K **21**
Longstock Clo. *Chine* ...4K **5**

Long Sutton. ...7D **24**
Lovegroves. *Chine* ...5J **5**
Love La. *Odi* ...2D **24**
(in two parts)
Loveridge Clo. *B'stoke* ...7C **12**
Lwr. Brook St. *B'stoke* ...4B **12**
Lwr. Chestnut Dri.
B'stoke ...6B **12**
Lowlands Rd. *B'stoke* ...6G **11**
Loyalty La. *Old B* ...3K **13**
Ludlow Clo. *B'stoke* ...4J **11**
Ludlow Gdns. *B'stoke* ...4K **11**
Lundy Clo. *B'stoke* ...7F **5**
Lune Clo. *B'stoke* ...4F **13**
Lupin Clo. *B'stoke* ...2G **19**
Lutyens Clo. *Lych* ...7H **5**
Lychpit. ...1H **13**
Lyde Clo. *Okly* ...1B **18**
Lyde Green. ...1H **7**
Lyford Rd. *B'stoke* ...3D **12**
Lymington Clo. *B'stoke* ...3H **19**
Lyn Ct. *B'stoke* ...4F **13**
Lyndhurst Dri. *B'stoke* ...4J **19**
Lynwood Gdns. *Hook* ...7A **8**
Lytton Rd. *B'stoke* ...4E **12**

Mabbs La. *H Wint* ...4J **9**
McCartney Wlk. *B'stoke* ...3J **19**
Madeira Clo. *B'stoke* ...7F **5**
Magnolia Ct. *B'stoke* ...7C **4**
Magnus Dri. *B'stoke* ...3H **19**
Magpie Clo. *B'stoke* ...2F **19**
Mahler Clo. *B'stoke* ...2B **20**
Majestic Rd. *B'stoke* ...4G **19**
Maldive Rd. *B'stoke* ...7F **5**
Malham Gdns. *B'stoke* ...5H **19**
Mallard Clo. *B'stoke* ...3F **19**
Malls Shop. Cen., The.
B'stoke ...4D **12**
Malmesbury Fields.
B'stoke ...2K **19**
Malshanger La. *Okly* ...5A **10**
Malta Clo. *B'stoke* ...7D **4**
Malvern Clo. *B'stoke* ...6G **11**
Manley James Clo. *Odi* ...6E **16**
Manor Clo. *B'stoke* ...4G **19**
Manor La. *Old B* ...3K **13**
Manor Rd. *Sher J* ...5A **4**
Mansfield Rd. *B'stoke* ...7A **12**
Maple Ct. *B'stoke* ...5H **11**
Maple Cres. *B'stoke* ...2D **12**
Mapledurwell. ...5C **14**
Maplehurst Chase.
B'stoke ...4H **19**
Maplewood. *Chine* ...5G **5**
Margaret Rd. *B'stoke* ...5K **11**
Marigold Clo. *B'stoke* ...2G **19**
Market Chambers.
B'stoke ...5D **12**
(off Church St.)
Market Pl. *B'stoke* ...5D **12**
Mark La. *B'stoke* ...5D **12**
Marlborough Gdns.
Okly ...7B **10**
Marlborough Trad. M.
Chine ...6F **5**
Marlowe Clo. *B'stoke* ...1E **12**
Marl's La. *B'stoke* ...3D **4**
Marshall Gdns. *B'stoke* ...2D **12**
Marshcourt. *Lych* ...1H **13**
Martin Clo. *B'stoke* ...2E **12**
Martins Wood. *Chine* ...5H **5**
Mary Rose Ct. *B'stoke* ...5B **12**
Mathias Wlk. *B'stoke* ...4K **19**
Matilda Dri. *B'stoke* ...3H **19**
Matthews Way. *Okly* ...1C **18**
Mattingley. ...1C **8**
Mattock Way. *Chine* ...5G **5**
Maw Clo. *B'stoke* ...2B **20**
Maybrook. *Chine* ...4H **5**
May Clo. *Old B* ...3A **14**

Mayfair Ho. *B'stoke* ...4D **12**
(off Festival Pl.)
Mayfield Ridge. *Hat W* ...5J **19**
Mayflower Clo. *Chine* ...6G **5**
Maynard's Wood. *Chine* ...6G **5**
May Pl. *B'stoke* ...5D **12**
May St. *B'stoke* ...4B **12**
Mead Hatchgate. *Hook* ...6A **8**
Meadowland. *Chine* ...5G **5**
Meadow La. *H Wint* ...2J **9**
Meadowridge. *Hat W* ...5J **19**
Meadow Rd. *B'stoke* ...7C **12**
Mead, The. *Old B* ...3K **13**
Medina Gdns. *Okly* ...1B **18**
Medway Av. *Okly* ...7B **10**
Medway Ct. *B'stoke* ...4F **13**
Melford Gdns. *B'stoke* ...7G **11**
Melrose Wlk. *B'stoke* ...1B **12**
Memorial Rd. *Hook* ...1A **16**
Mendip Clo. *B'stoke* ...6G **11**
Meon Rd. *Okly* ...1B **18**
Meon Wlk. *B'stoke* ...4E **12**
Mercer Clo. *B'stoke* ...5J **11**
Merlin Mead. *B'stoke* ...4F **19**
Merriatt Clo. *B'stoke* ...7D **12**
Merrileas Gdns. *B'stoke* ...2G **19**
Merrydown La. *Chine* ...6J **5**
Merryfield. *Chine* ...5G **5**
Merton Rd. *B'stoke* ...3C **12**
Middle Mead. *Hook* ...7A **8**
Middleton Gdns. *B'stoke* ...2D **12**
Midlane Clo. *B'stoke* ...7C **12**
Mildmay Ct. *Odi* ...7E **16**
Mildmay Ter. *H Wint* ...2K **9**
Milestones Mus. ...4A **12**
Milkingpen La. *Old B* ...3K **13**
Millard Clo. *B'stoke* ...2B **12**
Millennium Ct. *B'stoke* ...4B **12**
Mill La. *H Wesp* ...1F **7**
Mill La. *N War* ...5B **16**
Mill Rd. *B'stoke* ...1J **11**
Mill Vw. *Grey* ...7K **15**
Milton Clo. *B'stoke* ...1E **12**
Minden Clo. *Chine* ...6G **5**
Mitchell Av. *H Wint* ...3J **9**
Mitchell Gdns. *B'stoke* ...3J **19**
Monachus La. *H Wint* ...1K **9**
Monarch Clo. *B'stoke* ...4G **19**
Mongers Piece. *Chine* ...4J **5**
Moniton Est. *B'stoke* ...5H **11**
Monk Sherborne. ...4H **3**
Monk Sherborne Ho.
Monk S ...3H **3**
Monk Sherborne Rd.
Ramsd ...1D **2**
Monsanto Ho. *B'stoke* ...7H **5**
Montague Pl. *B'stoke* ...6D **12**
Montserrat Pl. *B'stoke* ...6E **4**
Montserrat Rd. *B'stoke* ...6E **4**
Moorfoot Gdns. *B'stoke* ...6H **11**
Moorhams Av. *B'stoke* ...4G **19**
Moorings, The. *B'stoke* ...4F **13**
Moor Vw. *Old B* ...2K **13**
Morgaston Rd. *Brmly* ...2K **3**
Morley Rd. *Chine* ...1C **20**
Morris Ri. *Chine* ...6G **5**
Morris St. *Hook* ...1J **15**
Morse Rd. *B'stoke* ...5A **12**
Mortimer Clo. *H Wint* ...4H **9**
Mortimer La. *B'stoke* ...4C **12**
Moscrop Ct. *B'stoke* ...5C **12**
Moulshay La. *Sher L* ...3A **6**
Mourne Clo. *B'stoke* ...5H **11**
Mozart Clo. *B'stoke* ...2A **20**
Mulberry Way. *Chine* ...5H **5**
Mull Clo. *Okly* ...7A **10**
Mullins Clo. *B'stoke* ...1D **12**
Munnings Clo. *B'stoke* ...6F **13**
Murrell Green. ...5E **8**
Murrell Grn. Bus. Pk.
Hook ...6E **8**
Murrell Grn. Rd. *H Wint* ...3E **8**
Musgrave Clo. *B'stoke* ...2K **19**

Musket Copse. *Old B* ...3J **13**
Myland Clo. *B'stoke* ...1E **12**

Napoleon Dri. *B'stoke* ...2J **11**
Nash Clo. *B'stoke* ...2D **12**
Nash Meadows. *S Warn* ...6A **24**
Nately Rd. *Grey* ...6H **15**
Nately Scures. ...2G **15**
Neath Rd. *B'stoke* ...4F **13**
Nelson Lodge. *B'stoke* ...2A **12**
Neville Clo. *B'stoke* ...7D **12**
Neville Ct. *B'stoke* ...2G **13**
New Bri. La. *B'stoke* ...4G **13**
Newbury Rd. Junct.
B'stoke ...2K **11**
Newfound. ...5C **10**
Newman Bassett Ho.
B'stoke ...3J **11**
New Mkt. Sq. *B'stoke* ...4D **12**
Newnham. ...7H **7**
Newnham La.
Old B & Newn ...1K **13**
Newnham Pk. *Hook* ...1K **15**
Newnham Rd. *Newn* ...1H **15**
New North Dri. *Sher L* ...1C **6**
New Rd. *B'stoke* ...4D **12**
New Rd. *Brmly* ...1C **4**
New Rd. *H Wint* ...2J **9**
New Rd. *Hook* ...1A **16**
New Rd. *N War* ...5C **16**
New St. *B'stoke* ...5D **12**
Nightingale Gdns.
B'stoke ...1J **11**
Nightingale Gdns. *Hook* ...7A **8**
Norden Clo. *B'stoke* ...3E **12**
Norden Ho. *B'stoke* ...3E **12**
Normanton Rd. *B'stoke* ...2D **12**
Norn Hill. *B'stoke* ...3E **12**
Norn Hill Clo. *B'stoke* ...3E **12**
Northgate Way. *B'stoke* ...4G **19**
NORTH HAMPSHIRE HOSPITAL.
...1A **12**
N. Waltham Rd. *Okly* ...3A **18**
North Warnborough. ...6C **16**
Norton Ho. *B'stoke* ...6J **11**
Norton Ride. *Lych* ...2H **13**
Norwich Clo. *B'stoke* ...3H **19**
Novello Clo. *B'stoke* ...3K **19**
Nursery Clo. *Chine* ...5J **5**
Nursery Clo. *Hook* ...6A **8**
Nursery Ter. *N War* ...5C **16**

Oak Clo. *Okly* ...1B **18**
Oak Clo. *B'stoke* ...4F **13**
Oakfields. *Lych* ...1H **13**
Oak Hanger Clo. *Hook* ...7B **8**
Oaklands. *H Wint* ...3J **9**
Oaklands Pk. *Hook C* ...2J **15**
Oaklands Way. *B'stoke* ...3J **11**
Oakland Ter. *H Wint* ...2K **9**
Oakley. ...1A **18**
Oakley La. *Okly* ...1A **18**
Oakley Pl. *H Wint* ...2J **9**
(off High St.)
Oakridge. ...2E **12**
Oakridge Cen. *B'stoke* ...2E **12**
Oakridge Ho. *B'stoke* ...2E **12**
Oakridge Rd. *B'stoke* ...2B **12**
Oakridge Towers. *B'stoke* ...2E **12**
Oak Tree Rd. *Hook* ...6B **8**
Oakwood. *Chine* ...5G **5**
(Crockford La.)
Oakwood. *Chine* ...5H **5**
(Hanmore Rd.)
Oasts, The. *Long S* ...6D **24**
Oban Clo. *Okly* ...7A **10**
Oceana Cres. *Hat W* ...6F **19**
Ochil Clo. *B'stoke* ...6H **11**

Every possible care has been taken to ensure that the information given in this publication is accurate and whilst the publishers would be grateful to learn of any errors, they regret they cannot accept any responsibility for loss thereby caused.

The representation on the maps of a road, track or footpath is no evidence of the existence of a right of way.

The Grid on this map is the National Grid taken from Ordnance Survey mapping with the permission of the Controller of Her Majesty's Stationery Office.